DISCOVERING THE UNITED STATES

Delaware

BY KATHY MACMILLAN

An Imprint of Abdo Publishing
abdobooks.com

abdobooks.com

Published by Abdo Publishing, a division of ABDO, PO Box 398166, Minneapolis, Minnesota 55439.

Printed in China.
052024
092024

Cover Photo: Shutterstock Images
Interior Photos: North Wind Picture Archives/Alamy, 4–5; Farlap/Alamy, 6 (top left); Aubrey Huggins/Alamy, 6 (top right); Jack Hong/Shutterstock Images, 6 (bottom left); Shutterstock Images, 6 (bottom right), 8, 26; Brian Kushner/Alamy, 10; Granger Historical Picture Archive, 12–13; Sarin Images/Granger Historical Picture Archive, 14; G. Fiume/Maryland Terrapins/Getty Images Sport/Getty Images, 17; Jason Smith/Getty Images for NASCAR/Getty Images Sport/Getty Images, 18; Bo Shen/Shutterstock Images, 20–21, 28 (bottom right); Edwin Remsberg/Alamy, 23; Leo Ang/iStockphoto, 24, 28 (bottom left); Red Line Editorial, 28 (top), 29

Editor: Marley Richmond
Series Designer: Katharine Hale

Library of Congress Control Number: 2023949341

Publisher's Cataloging-in-Publication Data

Names: MacMillan, Kathy, author.
Title: Delaware / by Kathy MacMillan
Description: Minneapolis, Minnesota: Abdo Publishing, 2025 | Series: Discovering the United States | Includes online resources and index.
Identifiers: ISBN 9781098293789 (lib. bdg.) | ISBN 9798384913054 (ebook)
Subjects: LCSH: U.S. states--Juvenile literature. | Delaware--History--Juvenile literature. | Northeastern States--Juvenile literature. | Physical geography--United States--Juvenile literature.
Classification: DDC 973--dc23

All population data taken from:
"Estimates of Population by Sex, Race, and Hispanic Origin: April 1, 2020 to July 1, 2022." *US Census Bureau, Population Division*, June 2023, census.gov.

CONTENTS

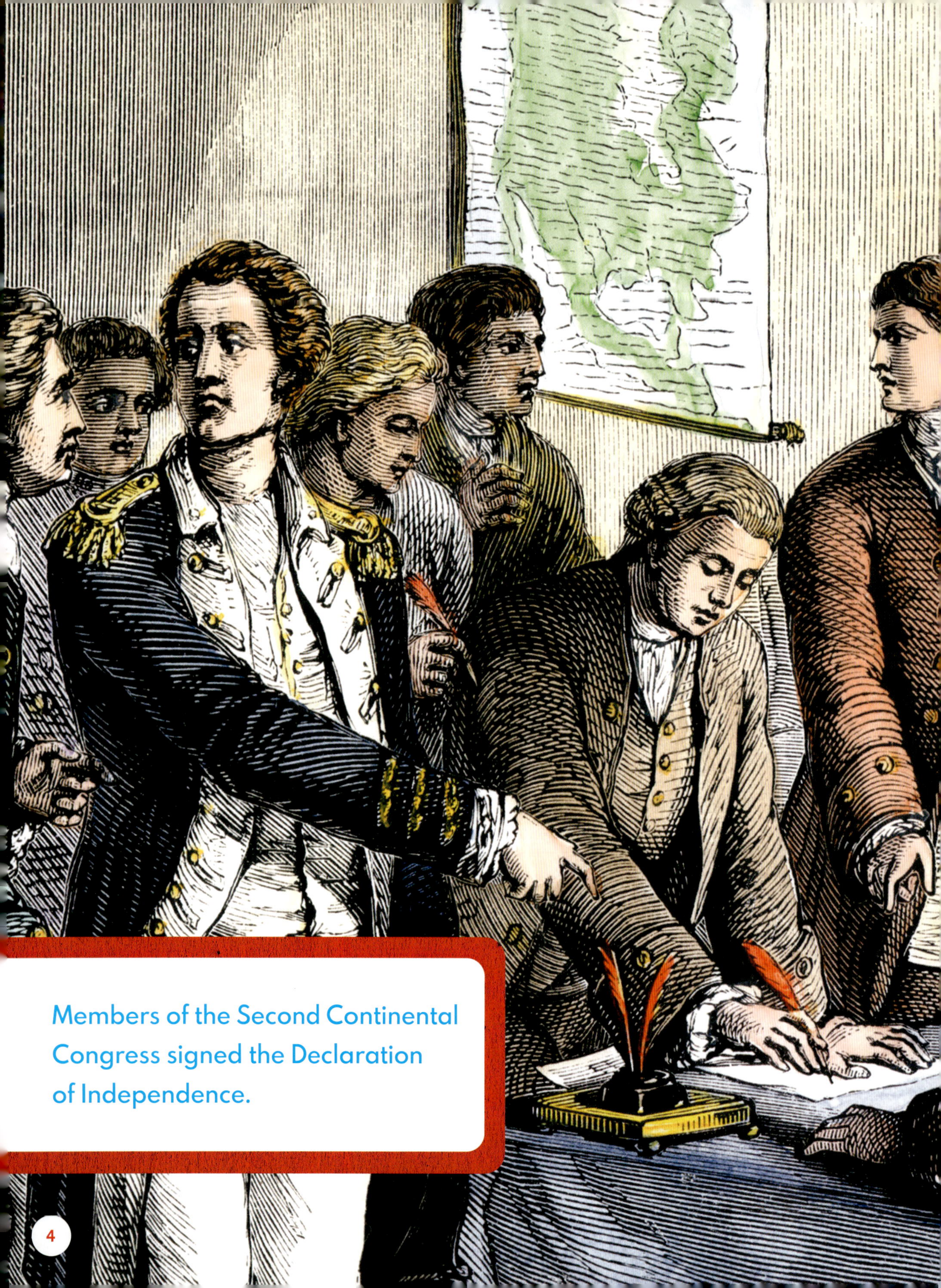

Members of the Second Continental Congress signed the Declaration of Independence.

CHAPTER 1

Small State, Big History

On the night of July 1, 1776, Caesar Rodney set out from his home in Dover, Delaware. A summer storm raged. Rodney was ill with cancer. But he had to return to the Second Continental Congress in Pennsylvania as quickly as possible.

Delaware Facts

DATE OF STATEHOOD
December 7, 1787

CAPITAL
Dover

POPULATION
1,018,396

AREA
2,489 square miles
(6,446 sq km)

STATE BIRD

Blue hen

STATE TREE

American holly

STATE FLOWER

Peach blossom

STATE MARINE ANIMAL

Horseshoe crab

Each US state has a different population, size, and capital city. States also have state symbols.

The United States was not yet a country. It was still part of Great Britain. Rodney was helping to decide if the United States would become independent. He was a

representative from Delaware. His vote was important. It would break a tie. Rodney wanted to vote for independence. He spurred his horse on through mud and lightning. It took him 14 hours to ride 80 miles (130 km) there. He arrived just in time to cast his vote on July 2. He still wore his riding boots and spurs. The United States declared independence from Great Britain on July 4, 1776.

Becoming Delaware

Delaware was part of the New York **colony** until 1682. Then it became part of the Pennsylvania colony. But it was hard for lawmakers to travel in such a big area of land. In 1704, Delaware set up its own government.

The Delaware state flag includes the date December 7, 1787. That was the day Delaware officially became the United States' first state.

Sand, Water, and Hills

Delaware sits on the East Coast of the United States. It is in the region called the South. It is bordered by Pennsylvania to the north.

New Jersey is to the northeast across Delaware Bay. The Atlantic Ocean is to the southeast. Maryland is to the south and west. Delaware is a small state. Only Rhode Island is smaller.

Most of Delaware sits on the low, flat Atlantic Coastal Plain. Delaware has many sandy beaches. It also has many marshes and streams. The northern part of the state has hills. These are the **foothills** of the Appalachian Mountains. The state's highest point is near the Pennsylvania state line. It is only 448 feet (137 m) above sea level.

Climate

Delaware has a moderate climate. It has four seasons. Winters are cold. Sometimes it snows.

About 25 percent of Delaware is covered in wetlands and marshes.

Summers are hot and humid. The ocean, rivers, and streams help keep Delaware's temperature from getting very high or very low. Delaware gets plenty of rain all year long. Plants such as orchids, milkweed, and **sedges** grow in Delaware's forests and marshes.

Trees in Delaware include oak, birch, ash, and maple trees. Delaware has many different animals. Red foxes, tortoises, squirrels, bats, and opossums can be seen around the state.

Explore Online

Visit the website below. What new information did you learn about Delaware that wasn't in Chapter One?

Office of the Governor, Kid's Corner

abdocorelibrary.com/discovering-delaware

Some American Indians traded with Europeans who came to Delaware.

The People of Delaware

People first came to Delaware's land more than 10,000 years ago. The Lenape were an American Indian people in this area. For thousands of years, they lived in farming communities. They farmed, fished, and hunted. Families lived in **longhouses**.

A British explorer named the state of Delaware after Virginia governor Thomas West, *pictured*. West's title was Baron De La Warr.

In the 1700s, the colonial government forced the Lenape to give up their land. They moved westward. The Nanticoke are related to the Lenape. Many Nanticoke people still live in Delaware. The tribe holds a powwow every year. This is a celebration of Nanticoke culture through singing, dancing, and food.

Delaware Today

Now, more than 1 million people live in Delaware. About 60 percent are white. Nearly 24 percent are Black. More than 4 percent are Asian. Less than 1 percent are American Indian. Almost 10 percent were born outside of the United States. More than half of Delaware's people live in the northern part of the state.

People in Delaware eat a lot of seafood. Fish and steamed crabs are popular. Many Delawareans like a breakfast meat called scrapple. Scrapple is made from pig scraps. The scraps are mixed with flour, cornmeal, spices, and maple syrup.

Delaware has no major professional sports teams. But Delawareans still love sports.

Many people cheer on teams at the University of Delaware. The school's teams are called the Fightin' Blue Hens. Famous athletes have also come from Delaware, such as Elena Delle Donne.

Working in Delaware

Many people in Delaware work for DuPont. DuPont started in 1802 as a gunpowder factory.

Delaware's Most Famous Resident

In 2021, Joe Biden became president of the United States. Long before that, he lived in Delaware. He was a US senator. He rode the train to Washington, DC, for work. Even as president, Biden kept two houses in Delaware.

Elena Delle Donne played basketball at the University of Delaware. She was later named the Most Valuable Player of the Women's National Basketball Association in 2015 and 2019.

Now it is a chemical company. DuPont has factories all over the world. But its main office is in Wilmington, Delaware.

DuPont used to make car paint. To advertise this, the company sponsored NASCAR driver Jeff Gordon.

Delaware has a lot of businesses for its small size. This is because the state has lower **taxes** for businesses than other states do. Lower taxes make it cheaper for businesses to be based in Delaware.

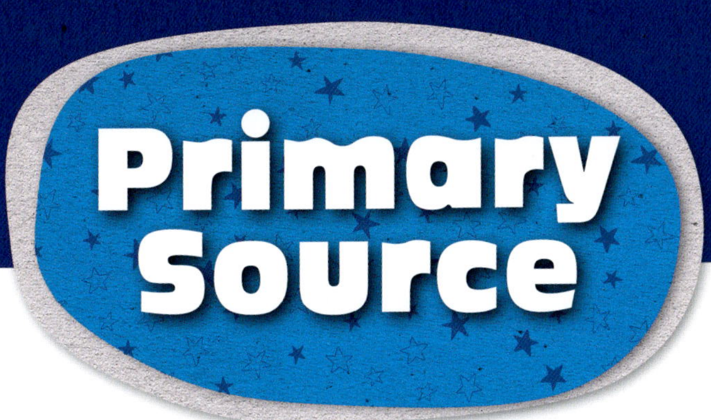

Traditional dances are an important part of Nanticoke powwows. Adrienne "Dancing Sparrow Eyes" Harmon said:

> I dance to promote awareness about my Native American culture. . . . We're letting people know we are still here.

Source: Suzanne Herel. "Meet the First Woman to Lead Delaware's Nanticoke Indian Tribe." *Delaware Today*, 15 Nov. 2021, delawaretoday.com. Accessed 27 Sept. 2023.

Comparing Texts

Think about the quote. Does it support the information in this chapter? Or does it give a different perspective? Explain how in a few sentences.

Wilmington sits between Brandywine Creek and the Christina River.

CHAPTER 3

Places in Delaware

Delaware has a few major cities. Wilmington is the largest city in the state. It is a port city along the Delaware River. Wilmington is the center of business in Delaware.

Wilmington has many historic landmarks. One is Old Swedes Church. It was built in 1698.

People still go to church there. Another is the Hagley Museum and Library. It sits on the site of the original DuPont gunpowder factory. Visitors can see how workers lived in the 1800s.

Dover is the capital of Delaware. It was founded in 1683. Dover Green was the center of the original town of Dover. An important event happened nearby. Delaware's representatives **ratified** the US Constitution on December 7, 1787. Delaware was the first colony to do so. As a result, it became the new country's first state.

Many NASCAR fans visit Dover Motor Speedway. This concrete racetrack is called the Monster Mile. It has many difficult turns.

Dover Motor Speedway can hold up to 58,800 fans for a NASCAR race.

Rehoboth Beach calls itself The Nation's Summer Capital. Around 3.5 million people visit the town each year.

More Places to See

In the summer, people gather at Rehoboth Beach. They swim and lie in the sun. They might also visit the boardwalk. The boardwalk was built in 1873. It has rides, arcades, shops, and restaurants.

Cape Henlopen State Park is nearby. Many birds and animals live among its large **dunes**. The park's Great Dune rises 80 feet (24 m) above sea level.

The Nanticoke Indian Museum has arrowheads, pottery, and traditional clothing.

Fort Miles

Inside Cape Henlopen State Park sits Fort Miles. This was an army base during World War II (1939–1945). Soldiers kept watch for German submarines. Now it is a museum. Visitors can see old anti-battleship guns. They can climb a tower and look over the Atlantic Ocean.

Fort Delaware has five sides and is surrounded by a moat.

Some of these items are from almost 10,000 years ago. They tell the story of Nanticoke culture.

Fort Delaware State Park sits on an island in the Delaware River. During the American Civil

War (1861–1865), it housed prisoners of war. Now visitors can learn about Delaware history. Birds such as herons, egrets, and ibis live on the island.

Delaware has lots to see, from beautiful beaches to rolling hills. It is sometimes called "Small Wonder." Though Delaware is tiny, it holds a big place in the history of the United States.

Further Evidence

Look at the website below. Does it give any new evidence to support Chapter Three?

Explore Historic Locations

abdocorelibrary.com/discovering-delaware

State Map

KEY

Capital
Park
City or town
Point of interest

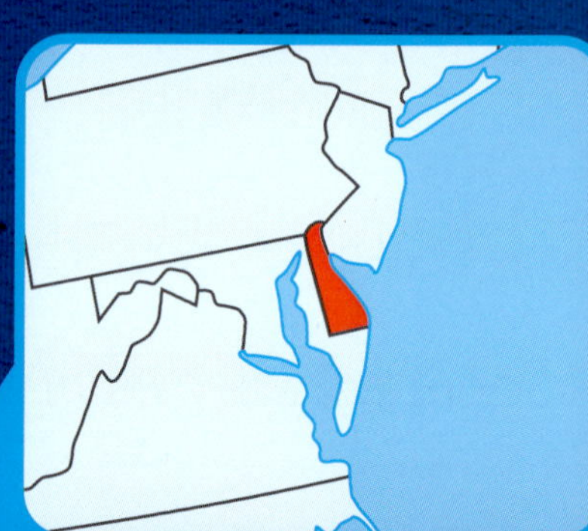

Rehoboth Beach

Wilmington

Delaware: The First State
Pennsylvania
Wilmington
Newark
Christina River
Fort Delaware
State Park
Chesapeake and
Delaware Canal
Middletown
New Jersey
N
W
E
S
Delaware River
Dover
Delaware Bay
Maryland
Cape Henlopen
State Park
Atlantic
Ocean
Lewes
Rehoboth Beach
Rehoboth Bay
Indian River Bay
Nanticoke Indian Museum
Bethany Beach
Fenwick
Island

Glossary

colony
an area that is controlled by another country

dune
a mound formed by wind pushing sand into large piles

foothills
a hilly area at the base of a mountain range

longhouses
long, low, one-room buildings made of wood and bark

ratified
officially approved

representative
a person who speaks or acts for a group

sedges
grasslike plants

taxes
money that businesses or people must pay to the government

Online Resources

To learn more about Delaware, visit our free resource websites below.

Visit **abdocorelibrary.com** or scan this QR code for free Common Core resources for teachers and students, including vetted activities, multimedia, and booklinks, for deeper subject comprehension.

Visit **abdobooklinks.com** or scan this QR code for free additional online weblinks for further learning. These links are routinely monitored and updated to provide the most current information available.

Learn More

Miller, Derek, Brian Fitzgerald, David King, and Kerry Jones Waring. *Delaware*. Cavendish Square, 2020.

The 50 States. DK, 2021.

Tieck, Sarah. *Delaware*. Abdo, 2020.

Index

About the Author

Kathy MacMillan is a writer, nationally certified American Sign Language interpreter, librarian, and signing storyteller. She writes picture books, children's nonfiction, middle grade and young adult fiction, and resource books for educators and librarians. She lives in Baltimore, Maryland. She camps at Delaware's Cape Henlopen State Park every summer.